YOU CHOOSE
BOOKS™

Westward Expansion

An Interactive History Adventure

by Allison Lassieur

Consultant:
Malcolm Rohrbough, Professor of History
University of Iowa
Author, *Days of Gold: The California Gold Rush
and the American Nation*

Capstone
press®

Mankato, Minnesota

You Choose Books are published by Capstone Press,
151 Good Counsel Drive, P.O. Box 669, Mankato, Minnesota 56002.
www.capstonepress.com

Library of Congress Cataloging-in-Publication Data
Lassieur, Allison.
    Westward expansion : an interactive history adventure / by Allison Lassieur.
    p. cm. — (You choose books)
    Summary: "Describes the people and events of the age of Manifest Destiny
and the American West. The reader's choices reveal the historical details from the
perspective of a traveler on the Oregon Trail, a laborer, or a Sioux warrior" — Provided
by publisher.
    Includes bibliographical references and index.
    ISBN-13: 978-1-4296-1359-0 (hardcover)
    ISBN-10: 1-4296-1359-9 (hardcover)
    ISBN-13: 978-1-4296-1766-6 (softcover pbk.)
    ISBN-10: 1-4296-1766-7 (softcover pbk.)
    1. West (U.S.) — History — 1848–1860 — Juvenile literature. 2. West (U.S.)
— History — 1860–1890 — Juvenile literature. 3. Frontier and pioneer life — West
(U.S.) — Juvenile literature. 4. United States — Territorial expansion — Juvenile
literature. I. Title. II. Series.
F593.L29 2008
978'.02 — dc22   2007034234

Editorial Credits
Megan Schoeneberger, editor; Juliette Peters, set designer; Gene Bentdahl, book
    designer; Wanda Winch, photo researcher; Danielle Ceminsky, illustrator

Photo Credits
Art Resource, N.Y./ Private Collection, 6; The Bridgeman Art Library International/©
Museum of the City of New York, USA/Across the Continent:'Westward the Course
of Empire Takes it's Way', pub. by Currier and Ives, New York, 1868 (colour litho),
Palmer, Frances Flora Bond (Fanny) (c.1812–76) (after), 10–11; Corbis, 44, 83;
Corbis/ Bettmann, 71, 99; Corbis/Francis G. Mayer, 79; Corbis/James L. Amos, 22;
Corbis/Lowell Georgia, 104; Corbis/PoodlesRock, 100; Courtesy of the Adirondack
Museum, 52; The Denver Public Library, Western History Collection, Joseph Collier,
C-107, 49; The Denver Public Library, Western History Collection, W. H. Jackson,
WHJ-10626, 25; The Denver Public Library, Western History Collection, W. H.
Jackson, WHJ-10641, 26; Getty Images/Hulton Archive/MPI, 97; Getty Images/
Hulton Archive/Otto Herschan, 69; iStockphoto/Getty Images/Hulton Archive/
MPI, 72; James P. Rowan, 24; Library of Congress, 41, 59, 75; New York Public
Library/Photography Collection, Miriam and Ira D. Wallach Division of Art, Prints
and Photographs, Astor, Lenox and Tilden Foundations, 102; North Wind Picture
Archives, 12, 38, 50, 63, 89; Scotts Bluff National Monument/William Henry Jackson
Collection, cover, 17, 33, 34; SuperStock, 64, 91; Union Pacific Museum, 66

1 2 3 4 5 6 13 12 11 10 09 08

TABLE OF CONTENTS

ABOUT YOUR ADVENTURE

YOU are living in America in the age of westward expansion. Settlers are pushing the border of the United States farther and farther west. Will you join them?

In this book, you'll explore how the choices people made meant the difference between life and death. The events you'll experience happened to real people.

Chapter One sets the scene. Then you choose which path to read. Follow the directions at the bottom of each page. The choices you make will change your outcome. After you finish one path, go back and read the others for new perspectives and more adventures.

YOU CHOOSE the path
you take through history.

Americans felt it was their right to settle in the West, even though American Indians already lived there.

Manifest Destiny

The West. The word sends a thrill through you. For some, the West is a place to search for gold and strike it rich. Others hunger for adventure in a wild and untamed place.

It is the mid-1800s, and an idea called "Manifest Destiny" grips the country. That's a big name for a big idea. Americans believe that the United States is meant to reach from the Atlantic Ocean to the Pacific Ocean. And nothing, not even the American Indians who already live there, can or will get in their way.

Turn the page.

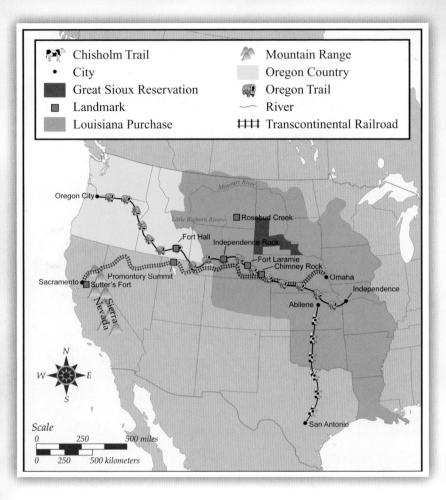

It isn't a new idea. Back in 1803, President
Thomas Jefferson made the Louisiana Purchase.
This huge section of land stretched from the
Mississippi River to the Rocky Mountains.
It doubled the size of the United States.

Soon, Americans took their first steps to explore the West. They brought back tales of a wild, rich land filled with promises.

Meanwhile, the U.S. population grew to more than 23 million people. Now, the East is crowded. Every day, Americans pack their wagons and move to the wide-open land of the West.

But Americans aren't the first people to live in the West. American Indians have lived there for hundreds of years. Now, they must share their hunting lands with white settlers. Except most settlers don't seem interested in sharing. Instead, they are taking the land away from the Indian tribes. They expect the Indians to live closer together in smaller areas.

Turn the page.

Americans built towns and railroads as they moved west.

Manifest Destiny affects everyone living during this time. Whether you join it or fight it, the shape of the United States is changing. Now is your chance to make your mark. What will you do?

➤ To travel west as a settler, turn to page **13**.

➤ To get an exciting job in the West, turn to page **45**.

➤ To fight for your land as a Lakota warrior,
turn to page **73**.

Families loaded as much as possible into their wagons before heading west.

CHAPTER 2

The Pioneers' Story

It is early March 1848. You and your family have sold everything but your clothes, a wagon, some oxen, and the cast-iron stove. You have said good-bye to your friends and neighbors. Mother and Father ride up front. You, your brother, and your sister climb into the wagon bed.

You are leaving your small Ohio farm behind and going west. Father is excited about the free land in the unsettled West. Any married person can claim 640 acres for free in Oregon Country. That's twice as much land as you own now, and no neighbors to crowd you!

13

Turn the page.

The three-week trip to Independence, Missouri, is an easy one. Independence is the "jumping off" place for most pioneers as they begin the long trip west. You've never seen such a busy town. You can barely think over the clatter of wagons and the shouts of hundreds of people rushing through the streets.

You and Father go to one of the many stores in Independence to buy supplies. "I'll need flour, bacon, coffee, sugar, and salt," Father says to the man standing behind the long wooden counter. You leave the store with almost 1,000 pounds of food.

Father parks the wagon outside town. Each day, more and more people arrive. The prairie is packed with pioneers and their wagons. Everyone is waiting for the grass to grow long enough for the animals to graze along the trail.

In late April, the grass is long and green. You can finally head west! You load the wagon and climb in. Father cracks the whip, and you follow the wagon train onto the trail.

The wagon is packed with food, the stove, and other supplies. The oxen plod slowly along as they pull the heavy load. You travel about 15 miles a day. It soon becomes clear that the wagon is too heavy. "It's too much for the oxen," Father says.

Other families begin dumping extra supplies. But Mother worries about running out of food. "I don't want my family to starve!" she cries.

"We'll still need to lighten the load somehow," Father says.

➤ To offer to walk to lighten the load, turn to page **16**.

➤ To get rid of some of your supplies, turn to page **17**.

You and your brother and sister get out of the wagon. "We can walk," you offer. "There's no need for the oxen to pull our weight too."

Father nods. "We'll give that a try," he says.

Walking instead of riding in the wagon lessens the load, but it doesn't solve the problem. The farther west you travel, the rockier the trail becomes. Father worries the heavy wagon won't survive the rough road. The oxen are exhausted. "We could break a wheel or an axle," Father says. "I'm sorry, but we need to dump something."

Wagon trains usually traveled single file along the Oregon Trail.

"We can buy more food when we get to the next fort," you suggest. You throw out several pounds of bacon and flour. Father unloads the cast-iron stove. Mother cries as you leave it behind. Cast-off furniture and supplies litter the trail.

You continue west, following the Platte River across the plains. The river is wide but shallow. The water is thick with mud. "It's too thick to drink and too thin to plow," Father says.

Turn the page.

Days fall into a pattern. Each morning, you eat breakfast, repack the wagon, and head out on the trail. After several hours, you stop for a lunch of cold beans and bacon before moving on. At suppertime, you stop and circle the wagons for the night. Your mother serves a hot meal of boiled rice with dried beef. After supper, you tell stories and sing songs around the campfire. You go to bed by 9:00 in the evening. Your bed is only a blanket on the hard ground, but you are too worn out to care.

A few weeks later, you wake up and hear crying and moaning. Something isn't right. You find Mother hunched over the breakfast fire. She looks pale and sick. "What is it?" you ask frantically.

"Cholera," she whispers. "Your brother and sister are sick too."

Cholera! There's no cure for this disease. You run to find Father, who is talking to the other men in the wagon train. "My daughter Sally is sick too," one man says. "We can't just leave them."

"We have to. We need to move on," another man says. "They may be dying," he continues, "but if we wait for them to die, we'll never make it to Oregon City before winter. Then we'll all be dead."

"We'll take the wagons ahead, and we'll choose a watcher, someone to stay behind with the dying people. The watcher will see that everyone gets a proper burial," suggests Sally's father.

Turn the page.

Father nods slowly in agreement. Your heart sinks. You can't leave your mother, brother, and sister behind. Maybe you should volunteer to be the watcher. But watching them die could be just as painful as leaving them behind. Either way, your heart is broken.

➤ *To volunteer to stay behind, go to page **21***.

➤ *To leave with the wagon train, turn to page **23***.

Father has the same idea. "I'll stay with them," you both say.

The men nod. A young man offers to drive Father's wagon. "The trail is so rough. You'll be able to travel faster on foot," he says.

The healthy travelers bid tearful good-byes to their dying loved ones. They quietly board their wagons. Dust rises behind them as they drive away.

Father begins the backbreaking task of digging graves. You stay with the sick to offer comfort. There's nothing else you can do. Within hours, your brother and sister are dead. Mother and Sally die sometime in the night.

Turn the page.

Graves of pioneers who died along the trail can still be found today.

The next morning, your head feels fuzzy, you're thirsty, and you have terrible stomach cramps. Cholera!

At least Father is still healthy. He waits with you, holding your hand. The sun rises, painting a glorious sunset across the prairie sky. Birds sing. You listen to their chirps as your life slowly fades away. Father will have to go west without you.

THE END

To follow another path, turn to page 11.
To read the conclusion, turn to page 101.

22

Sally's father steps forward. "I will stay," he says.

It feels like your heart is being torn from your chest, but you have no other choice. Your mother, brother, and sister would want you to keep going. Grimly, you and your father climb into the wagon and drive away.

After a few days, Sally's father catches up with the group. He tells you your mother, brother, and sister died in their sleep. He buried them and left stones as grave markers.

Turn the page.

The wagon train continues on at a good pace. In early June, you spot a tall column of rock standing in the distance. "Chimney Rock!" you shout. Three days later, you finally pass the landmark.

Spring turns to summer, but you lose count of the days. Grief weighs you down like a heavy stone.

Chimney Rock still stands in present-day Nebraska.

People often climbed Independence Rock and carved their names into it.

In early July, the wagon train stops for lunch by Independence Rock. It looks a bit like a giant turtle covering the flat prairie. You are relieved to reach the landmark by July 4. Any later, and you might not reach Oregon before winter.

Beyond Independence Rock, you reach the South Pass, a flat plain about 20 miles wide. You cross river after river. Each day blends into the next.

Turn the page.

Fort Hall was an important supply stop for westward settlers.

In early August, the wagon train arrives at Fort Hall just inside Oregon Territory. Hundreds of settlers pass through this large trading post every day. The wagon train decides to rest here for a few days. Father is restless, though. He wants to continue on without stopping. A few others agree with him. You'd like a rest, but you also want to get to Oregon City soon.

❧ To stop with the rest of the wagon train, go to page **27**.

❧ To continue on, turn to page **33**.

"It's best to stay with the large group," you say. Father agrees with you.

The next day, you and Father talk to other men at the crowded trading post. "I'm telling you, California is the place to be," one man says.

"Gold everywhere! Why, I heard you can't hardly walk down the street without kicking a nugget of gold," another man says.

"A bunch of us are going to California instead of Oregon. We're going to be rich! You can join us if you like," the first man says to Father.

California! You can tell by the look on Father's face that he is thinking about changing plans.

➻ To stick with your plan to go to Oregon, turn to page **28**.

➻ To try California, turn to page **29**.

Father thinks for a while and shakes his head. "No, let's keep going to Oregon City," he says.

You spend several days at Fort Hall. You stock up on supplies, repair wagons, and enjoy your first taste of Pacific salmon.

In mid-August, the wagon train begins the last leg of the long trip. You follow the Snake River to Farewell Bend. After several days, you reach the Blue Mountains. The oxen struggle for days to pull the wagon over the steep, rocky hills.

Nights grow colder as you near the Cascade Mountains. You worry that snow is on its way. But the weather holds, and in late September, you reach a green valley dotted with houses. Oregon City! You feel like crying with relief. You made it here alive.

Turn to page **38.**

The lure of life in a warm place is enough for Father to change his mind. You're going to California instead.

The next day, you leave Fort Hall and head southwest. Soon, the wagon train arrives at a fork in the trail. One fork leads west, and the other leads south. A note is stuck to a stick between the two roads. Eagerly, you read the note aloud: "Go south for Lassen's Cutoff. Good road."

A shortcut sounds great to you. But others don't trust the note. There is talk that the way south is harsh and rugged. Which do you choose?

➤ To take Lassen's Cutoff, turn to page **30**.

➤ To take the longer, more common route, turn to page **35**.

You follow Lassen's Cutoff. For a week, the trail is easy. Then the trail suddenly ends at the top of a hill. A deep, thick forest stretches as far as you can see.

"If Lassen made it through, so can we," Father says. Cutting a road through the forest is a struggle. Some days, you work 10 hours to cut only 1 mile of trail.

Almost three weeks later, you emerge from the forest, cursing the "shortcut" that cost you so much time. It's the beginning of October. You hope to cross the Sierra Nevada mountain range before the first snow, but you'll have to travel quickly.

The next weeks are a blur of hunger and endless days. The weather grows colder. Then one day, you see the Sierra Nevada mountain range. The brand-new town of Sacramento is on the other side. Your new life awaits you!

The night before you begin your crossing, it begins to snow. In the morning, there are several feet of snow on the ground.

➤ To stay here, make a camp, and hope you survive the winter, turn to page **32**.

➤ To try to get over the mountain before the next snowstorm, turn to page **40**.

It's clear that you're never going to make it over the mountain before winter hits. The people in the wagon train build makeshift cabins to wait out the winter.

One by one, Father butchers the oxen, but it's still not enough. You eat shoe leather, bark, twigs, and leaves — anything to keep you alive. Somehow, you and Father manage to survive the winter. Almost everyone else starves or freezes to death.

In early spring, a rescue party arrives at your camp. One by one, they gather the few survivors and lead you out of the mountains. You weep with joy and relief. Your terrible ordeal is over. Soon, you reach Sutter's Fort.

Turn to page 36.

You leave Fort Hall the next day. You follow the Snake River, passing American Falls, Shoshone Falls, and Twin Falls. Two weeks later, you reach Three Island Crossing. You don't have to cross here. But this side of the river is dry and bare. Across the river, the valley is lush and green. Crossing the river is risky. Some people say it is the most dangerous river crossing of the whole trip. What choice will you make?

Settlers used three small islands as stepping stones to cross the Snake River.

➤ *To not cross the river, turn to page* **34**.

➤ *To cross the river, turn to page* **37**.

The Barlow Road cut through thick forests and steep hills to go around Mount Hood.

"Let's stay to the south," Father says.

In late August, you enter the Blue Mountains. The nights are chilly. Snow will be falling soon. You are glad you didn't waste any time at Fort Hall.

Finally, you reach Barlow Road. For a $5 toll, you take the road around Mount Hood and into the Willamette Valley. Beyond the valley is Oregon City.

*Turn to page **38**.*

"Let's play it safe and take the common route," you suggest. Everyone agrees.

The wagon train pushes west toward California. You must make it over the Sierra Nevada mountain range before the first snowfall. You begin to cross the mountains in early November.

You make it through the mountains and into California just in time. You look back and see a blizzard brewing. You wonder what would have happened if you had gotten stuck in that terrible storm.

You and Father go directly to Sutter's Fort near the American River.

Turn to page 36.

You and Father spend two weeks at Sutter's Fort. You've never seen such a place. Everywhere you look, you see mud and dirty men with pickaxes and shovels.

You hear tales of men striking it rich in the gold fields. You are anxious to give mining a try. But one day, Father comes to you. "I've got a better idea," he says. "We can get rich without ever lifting a shovel. We can sell mining supplies."

You're not so sure about the idea. Finding gold could make you an overnight millionaire. How could opening a shop make you rich? But you think about Father's idea for a few hours.

➜ *To try mining, turn to page* **41**.

➜ *To open a store, turn to page* **43**.

"It doesn't look too deep," Father says. "Let's give it a try."

You send the oxen across. As they swim, they struggle in the fast current, but they make it. You and Father load everything in the wagon bed and start to float across the river.

Just beyond the first island, the wagon slams against an unseen sandbar. You fall into the clear water. It is deeper than it looked, and the current pulls you under.

With all your strength, you try to swim to safety. The current is too strong. Finally, you give up. You came so close to Oregon City, but you don't make it. You and Father drown in the Snake River.

THE END

To follow another path, turn to page 11.
To read the conclusion, turn to page 101.

Oregon City is your new home. Father finds a piece of land with streams, forests, and wide fields. He registers his claim with the town, and the land is yours.

Father and several other men cut down trees and build the cabin. With the extra help, it doesn't take long to finish. It has one room, with a loft for you to sleep in. The floor is dirt. Father promises you a much nicer house made of sawed lumber as soon as a sawmill comes to town.

Pioneers cut down trees to build log cabins.

One evening, Father builds the first fire in the new fireplace. You miss your mother, brother, and sister terribly. You watch the fire. "What happens next?" you ask.

"Over the winter, I'll hunt for food. This spring, we'll plant our first crop. You'll be going to school too. It'll be hard work with just the two of us. Are you ready for it?"

Your pioneer adventure didn't turn out exactly as you thought it would. But you're determined to make this new life work.

"I'm ready for anything!" you tell him.

THE END

To follow another path, turn to page 11.
To read the conclusion, turn to page 101.

Being so close to Sacramento, you can't bear to wait until spring. To make travel easier, you leave everything behind except what you can carry on your back. Then, you head up the mountain. You struggle through snow up to your waist.

By dark, you're only halfway up the mountain. As your exhausted group makes a camp, it starts to snow again. It soon becomes a blizzard. You know there is no way you will survive the cold. You wrap yourself in a blanket and huddle under a tree. Somehow, death doesn't scare you. After everything you've been through, it seems like a relief.

THE END

To follow another path, turn to page 11.
To read the conclusion, turn to page 101.

Miners used pans to collect gold from rivers and streams during the gold rush.

"Let's mine for gold," you beg Father the next morning. "We're going to get lucky. I can just feel it!"

Turn the page.

Father finally agrees to give it a try. You even find a little gold your very first day. But as the months pass, more and more miners show up. The fields get crowded, and the gold becomes harder to find. You find just enough gold to get by, but you never do strike it rich.

THE END

To follow another path, turn to page 11.
To read the conclusion, turn to page 101.

"Gold mining is for fools," Father says. The more you think about it, the more you agree. Father purchases a large canvas tent and a supply of shovels, axes, and other tools. Business is booming. Father can't keep items in stock.

The next year, Father marries a widow named Alice. She's nice, and you're glad to see Father happy again. You go to school. It's not the life you expected when you left your old home. You still miss your mother, brother, and sister. But you know they'd be pleased that you survived the journey and have a new life in California.

THE END

To follow another path, turn to page 11.
To read the conclusion, turn to page 101.

Burned-out battlefields were common in Louisiana and throughout the South after the Civil War (1861–1865).

CHAPTER 3

Working in the Wild West

It's 1868, three years after the end of the Civil War. When the Civil War began, you proudly volunteered for the Confederate army. For four long years, you fought battle after bloody battle. And for nothing, it seems. The Confederacy lost.

When the war ended, you returned to your farm in Louisiana. You learned that you are the only one left of your family. Union soldiers burned your fields and took everything. All that's left is the house and the land.

Turn the page.

One afternoon in town, you hear that the Union Pacific railroad is looking for strong men to help build a railroad across the country. Before you have time to think about this information, a friend waves to you.

"I'm going to Texas to help with a cattle drive," he says

"What's that?" you ask.

"Some big cattle barons want to bring their cattle from Texas up north to sell them. They need cowboys to herd the cattle."

No matter which job you choose, you will be able to get out of Louisiana for good.

➤ *To join the cattle drive, go to page 47.*
➤ *To work on the railroad, turn to page 51.*

You head for south Texas. You arrive at a dusty Texas town called San Antonio. There's an air of excitement in town.

You stand in the street, wondering what to do. A dark-haired man with a neatly trimmed beard approaches you. "You look lost, stranger," he says kindly. He reaches out to shake your hand. "I'm Charlie Goodnight."

You've heard of this man. He's a famous cowboy. You tell him that you're new in town. "Joseph McCoy's outfit is hiring cowboys," Goodnight says. He points to a boarding house. "Go in there, and they'll fix you right up."

"Thank you," you say.

Goodnight shakes your hand again. "Good luck," he says. Then he disappears into the crowd.

Turn the page.

You enter the small, dimly lit building.
A man in a tall hat and muddy boots sits at
a table. "Are you Joseph McCoy? I'm here for
the cowboy job," you say.

The man nods. He looks you up and down.
"Can you ride?" McCoy asks.

"Yes, I can ride," you reply.

"We're driving these cattle to my stockyards
in Abilene, Kansas. I'll give you $35 a month,"
McCoy says.

Three days later, you ride out to find the
trail boss. He's a tall, rough man by the name
of Smith. "Now look here," he says. "I need a
volunteer." He scans the group until his gaze
settles on you. "You," he says. "You'll be a
pointer. Pointers lead the herd during the day.
At night, the pointers pick out the place where
the herd will stop and rest."

Cowboys rode on horseback to round up cattle.

The days on the trail are all the same. Each morning, you eat a breakfast of biscuits and beans while the cattle graze. Once breakfast is done, you round up the herd and move on.

At the end of the day, you take turns finding a camping place. When you find a spot with clean water and grass, you circle the herd, bringing the animals closer together. Once the herd is together and quiet, then you and the rest of the cowboys can eat supper and relax.

Turn the page.

Cowboys took turns sleeping and keeping watch over the cattle at night.

One night while you are on watch, the cattle become restless. You think you see a group of shadows at one end of the herd. Are they Indians? Or is it just your imagination?

→ To go check it out, turn to page **54**.

→ If you think it's nothing, turn to page **64**.

The idea of working on the railroad fills you with excitement. The Union Pacific will be building a rail from east to west. Another company, the Central Pacific, is building a rail from west to east. The two will meet somewhere in the middle, completing the first transcontinental railroad across the country.

You travel north by steamboat on the Missouri River to Omaha, Nebraska. At the Union Pacific offices, several other men are waiting to sign up. At the head of the line, you see a tall man with a bushy moustache talking to an older gentleman.

"Who are they?" you ask the person next to you in line.

"You don't know them?" the man replies.

Turn the page.

Thomas Durant ran the Union
Pacific railroad.

"The young one is Grenville Dodge, the chief engineer of this operation. The older man is Union Pacific's vice president, Thomas Durant."

You're hired as a laborer. You will receive $35 a month with room and board. The next day, you and dozens of other new workers board large wagons and set out for the construction site.

When you get there, you can't believe what you see. It's hot, dusty, and loud. Large gangs of men are laying track. Two men pull a rail from a small wagon and run with it to the end of the track. The leader shouts a command, and the men drop the rail into place. It only takes 30 seconds to lay each rail.

Soon, a large man with a booming voice calls all the new workers together. "Listen up," he says. "We need strong backs to load the rails and materials and take them to the crews. I also need someone who knows something about bridge construction."

You could do either job, you think. For which job should you volunteer?

→ To build bridges, turn to page **57**.

→ To load supplies, turn to page **66**.

You grab your rifle and gallop toward the shadows. Sure enough, it is a small group of Indians. When they see you, they jump on their horses and ride away.

You tell Smith what you saw. "Good work," he tells you. He immediately doubles the guards for the night. "Indians sometimes try to stampede the cattle. Then they demand a reward for returning them," he explains.

It begins to rain the next day and doesn't let up. When you reach the Red River, the brown water churns as it rushes past.

Smith eyes the river. "It's not as bad as it looks," he says finally. "It won't be a problem for the cattle to cross." You're not so sure, however.

✦ To suggest waiting for the night, go to page **55**.

✦ To cross the river, turn to page **60**.

"I think we should wait. Better to be running late than to lose too many cattle," you say to Smith.

After one more day, the rain finally stops. You wait a few more days for the river to go down. When it is time to cross, Smith takes the lead. "Follow me closely," he said. "This river's full of quicksand." About halfway across, a few cattle get stuck on a sandbar. You get off your horse and wade into the river to get them moving again. Before long, all the cattle are safely across the river.

The Red River is the boundary between Texas and Indian Territory. You travel through the territory for several weeks on your way to Kansas.

Turn the page.

When you cross the border into Kansas, Smith gives a warning. "Look out for sheep ranchers. They don't like our herds passing through their lands. They've been known to stampede our cattle to scare us away."

"If they mess with us, we'll just stampede their sheep," another cowboy threatens. "That'll teach them a lesson."

The next day, you see a line of strangers on horseback. Sure enough, they're sheep ranchers. They demand to talk to someone in charge.

Behind you, a few cowboys sneak away. They're going to stampede the ranchers' sheep. Should you join them?

❧ To stampede the sheep, turn to page **61**.

❧ To talk to the men, turn to page **62**.

You like building bridges. Your crew works miles ahead of the rest of the railroad crew. You must finish the bridges before the construction crews can lay the tracks.

Your crew starts construction on a large bridge over a deep ravine. It's a tricky job. The wind blows hard through the cliffs, making the bridge sway dangerously. One wrong decision and the whole thing will collapse.

One day, you notice some loose soil under the bridge supports. It's not uncommon to find this kind of problem, so you order your men to dig it out. A few hours later, they say they are finished. The area looks stable now.

➤ If you want to double-check, turn to page **58**.

➤ If you think it's safe, turn to page **67**.

"I don't trust anything out here," you mutter as you grab a shovel and start to dig. Sure enough, a few feet down you hit a patch of unstable ground. You order your crew to repair the area.

Unstable ground and lazy workers aren't your only concerns, though. One evening, soldiers ride into your camp. "What's the problem?" you ask in a friendly voice.

"I'm John Gibbon," the leader replies. "My men and I were hired by the Union Pacific to guard workers from Indian attacks. For your safety, you are to return to the main work area at once."

The railroad is being built through Cheyenne and Lakota Sioux hunting grounds, and the Indians are very angry at the railroad. You haven't seen any Indians yourself, though.

John Gibbon led a group of soldiers hired to protect railroad workers from Indian attacks.

"Well, we can't leave until the bridge is finished, sir," you reply.

"You can stay if you want," Gibbon replies. "But I can't be responsible for your men's safety if you do." What do you do?

→ To stay and finish your work, turn to page **68**.

→ To go back and wait until the threat is over, turn to page **69**.

Slowly, you and the other cowboys drive the cattle into the rushing water. A few cattle lose their footing and are swept downriver. The rest of the terrified herd stampedes straight into the water!

You charge into the water to save a small calf. Your horse's feet are swept out from under him, and you plunge into the dirty, cold water. Your head hits a rock with a sickening crunch, and you drown in the icy river.

For some, being a cowboy is a life of adventure. But for you, it brings only an early death in the Wild West.

THE END

To follow another path, turn to page 11.
To read the conclusion, turn to page 101.

You decide to join the stampede. The trail boss rides forward to speak to the farmers. Meanwhile, you and the other cowboys quietly ride around the herd. At first, the conversation seems friendly. Then you hear shouting.

With a shout, the cowboys ride furiously toward the sheep. The angry ranchers pull out their guns and open fire. As you feel a bullet tear through your chest, you realize that this wasn't such a good idea after all.

THE END

To follow another path, turn to page 11.
To read the conclusion, turn to page 101.

You ride up to Smith as he's talking to the farmers and sheep ranchers. With a nod from the trail boss, you address the restless crowd.

"Gentlemen," you say in your friendliest voice. "We are interested in buying flour, fruits, vegetables, and other supplies from you. I'm sure other cattle drives will need those supplies in the future. What do you say?"

The farmers and the sheep ranchers agree. You and several cowboys go to nearby farms, buying as much fresh fruit and vegetables as you can carry. You pay the farmers more than what they ask. That night, the cowboys enjoy a fine stew made with fresh ingredients, a rare treat.

A week later, you arrive in Abilene with most of the cattle healthy and ready for sale.

In Abilene, cowboys herded cattle into box cars to be taken to market.

Just a few years ago, Abilene was a speck on the map. Now there are stores, hotels, and gambling halls. There's so much to do and see that you almost don't know where to start!

That night, you watch the sun set over Abilene. You realize that the cowboy life is for you.

THE END

To follow another path, turn to page 11.
To read the conclusion, turn to page 101.

You hear some laughter and recognize the voices of some of the other cowboys. You relax. "My eyes are playing tricks on me," you whisper to yourself.

Suddenly, you hear a rifle shot. It was Indians you saw!

The cattle bellow and start to run. Stampede! You frantically try to round up the cattle, but many get away.

Rounding up stampeding cattle was not an easy task.

Later that day, several Indians show up leading a dozen cattle. They demand a reward for returning the animals. Smith is forced to trade food and other supplies in exchange for the cattle.

Then he calls for you. Smith hands you your pay. "Get out of here and don't come back," he growls. "You're a sorry excuse for a cowboy."

Disappointed, you wander back toward Louisiana. You don't know where else to go. You're sad that the cowboy life didn't work out. But you miss home too. Maybe you'll head back to your old farm. It's not much, but it's all you've got.

THE END

To follow another path, turn to page 11.
To read the conclusion, turn to page 101.

It took several crews to lay railroad tracks.

You and your crew pile rails, spikes, bolts, and other materials onto a railroad cart. A horse pulls the filled cart to the end of the last pair of rails. There, another crew lays down the rails. A third crew hammers the rails into place. As soon as all the supplies are unloaded, the empty cart is moved off the track. The horse pulls the cart back to your crew, so you can load it up again.

Turn to page **70.**

"Continue!" you order the workers.

The work goes quickly, and in no time a maze of timbers held together by iron bolts rises in the ravine. The timbers sway in the wind just as you thought they would. But you believe the bridge is very strong, even though it looks flimsy.

Soon, it's the last day of work on the bridge. That afternoon, you climb to the top of the bridge to check the progress. You're ready to sign off on the project when a huge gust of wind whips through the ravine. The bridge shudders. Far below, you see a sight that horrifies you. The section of ground where the loose soil had been begins to shift. Another gust of wind hits the bridge. As the bridge collapses, you are flung out into the air. You fall helplessly to your death.

67

THE END

To follow another path, turn to page 11.
To read the conclusion, turn to page 101.

"We haven't seen any Indians here," you say finally. "I think it's safe enough to finish."

Late the next evening, you're awakened by the sound of gunfire and yelling. Attack! You jump up, grab your rifle, and run out of your tent. Just then, more than 100 Lakota and Cheyenne warriors gallop into camp. Arrows whiz past as you aim and fire. One warrior falls from his horse in a heap at your feet. Suddenly, you feel a sharp pain in your arm. You've been hit! You fall to the dusty ground.

After what feels like forever, the fight ends. You lift your head and look around. Bodies lie all around you. Your arm aches, but you will recover. You feel lucky to be alive.

THE END

To follow another path, turn to page 11.
To read the conclusion, turn to page 101.

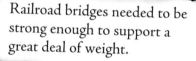

Railroad bridges needed to be strong enough to support a great deal of weight.

Reluctantly, you follow the guards back to the main camp. Two days later, you hear that Gibbon and his men drove off Indians near your bridge. You're glad you listened to him. Several days later, you return with your crew to finish the bridge.

Turn the page.

The work on the railroad continues for another year, and you're never bored. You enjoy the freedom of the open land and the pleasure of a hard job, done well.

In the spring of 1869, the two railroads are almost complete. Finally, on May 10, 1869, the two great rails meet at Promontory Summit, Utah. There is a happy mood in the camp.

Leland Stanford, the president of the Central Pacific, and Thomas Durant, the vice president of the Union Pacific, arrive. Stanford and Durant drive a ceremonial golden spike into the railroad. When that is complete, two huge locomotives slowly chug forward. One comes from the east, and the other comes from the west. They inch forward until they are almost touching.

![Crews gathered for a photograph after the completion of the Transcontinental Railroad.]

Crews gathered for a photograph
after the completion of the
Transcontinental Railroad.

You and your men climb on top of one of the
locomotives as a photographer takes pictures.
You almost can't believe that the work is done
and that you're part of such an historic moment.

THE END

To follow another path, turn to page 11.
To read the conclusion, turn to page 101.

Buffalo were once common on the Great Plains.

CHAPTER 4

The Warrior's Story

It is 1875, and you are a young member of the Lakota Sioux tribe. For generations, your people have lived on the Great Plains. The Lakota were once the most powerful tribe in the land. Lakota lands stretched thousands of miles. Buffalo, rabbits, and game birds were plentiful for hunting.

Many years ago, your tribe and the white settlers were friends. Your grandfather told you that the tribe had treaties of friendship with the U.S. government. In 1868, the U.S. government gave your people the Great Sioux Reservation in Dakota Territory. They promised that the land would belong to the Lakota forever.

Turn the page.

But the government broke its promise. Gold was discovered in the Black Hills. Now, settlers are coming onto the reservation land to dig for gold. They are taking land your family has lived on for generations. You feel betrayed. Many Lakota feel the same way.

But today you are not thinking much about white settlers and their promises. It is time for the summer buffalo hunt.

The buffalo give you everything you need. Their skins give you the tepees in which you live. Their fur keeps you warm in winter. Their meat gives you food. Without buffalo, your people wouldn't survive.

Lakota Sioux lived in small camps and moved often.

Women and children pack for the journey to the hunting grounds. You will be following the herds for several weeks. By the time the hunt is over, you hope to have enough buffalo to last the winter.

The journey is filled with laughter and fun. After a week of travel, you arrive at your hunting grounds.

Turn the page.

A terrible sight greets your eyes. Hundreds of buffalo carcasses litter the prairie. They have been skinned, and their heads are gone. The air is black with flies. Thousands of pounds of meat are rotting and wasted.

"White hunters," the rumor goes through the crowd. You are filled with anger.

"What if the buffalo killing continues? How will we live?" you cry.

"You must let this go," an old woman near you says.

➻ To form a raiding party and attack, go to page 77.

➻ To swallow your anger and continue the hunt, turn to page 78.

"We must strike now," you yell, waving your gun in the air. Several other warriors join your raiding party. You mount your horses and gallop out of the camp. It is not long before you find a large group of hunters camped nearby.

When the sun goes down, you ride to the hunters' camp. You quietly climb to the top of a hill. The men are camped beside a huge pile of buffalo skins lying in the dirt. The smell of rot and waste almost makes you sick.

As the night drags on, the hunters drop off to sleep. When the time is right, you all jump on your horses and attack.

Turn to page 84.

"I understand the wisdom of waiting," you tell the others. You bow your head. "I will focus now on hunting buffalo."

After two days, the band finds the buffalo herd. The massive herd of shaggy animals covers the plains to the horizon. It will be a good hunt.

Early the next morning, the hunt begins. You and the other hunters quietly approach the edges of the herd. You rush forward aiming and shooting. You hit a buffalo and it falls to the ground. The air is filled with shouts of your friends and the bellowing and thunder of the stampeding herd.

Great Plains Indians hunted buffalo for food, clothing, and shelter.

You look forward to many more days of hunting, feasting, and celebrating a good hunt. You're grateful to the buffalo for providing your people with food and shelter.

Turn the page.

One morning, you hear a shout from the camp guard. A group of white soldiers is approaching the camp. The sight of the uniformed soldiers fills you with fear. Time after time, the whites have broken their promises.

The soldiers ride to the center of your camp. You and the other warriors surround them. No one moves. The soldiers watch your group closely. You watch them just as closely. There is no trust between you.

Then one of the soldiers calls out, "We come in peace." Their leader rides forward and asks to speak to the chief.

Your chief, Sitting Bull, is visiting a neighboring Lakota camp, but you and a few other warriors step forward.

"We are here to invite you to a meeting," the soldier begins.

A few of your people understand English. They quietly translate the soldier's words as he speaks.

"The U.S. government wants to buy more land from you. At this meeting, we will come to an agreement on the terms of this sale. We are asking for representatives of all the Sioux on the Great Reservation to come."

A murmur goes through the crowd as the soldier's words sink in. "We do not want to sell our lands," you say. "The government gave us this reservation. You cannot take our land away." Many people behind you nod in agreement.

Turn the page.

The soldiers look angry. "It doesn't matter. The government wants the land. The meeting will be held this fall. You must be there." The soldiers get back on their horses and gallop away.

"A meeting to take our land away!" you say. "I will die before I let our lands be taken!" The band agrees with you.

Sitting Bull returns to camp and learns about the meeting with the white soldiers. When the time comes, he travels to the meeting. When he returns, he calls for the band to come to the center of the camp.

"The white soldiers want our land," Sitting Bull says. "We must fight for our right to move freely and hunt the buffalo as we wish, as our ancestors have," he continues. "But we will wait. We will go to war in the spring."

Sitting Bull urged the Lakota to resist the westward expansion of the United States.

Spring? Your life, and the lives of everyone you love, is at stake. You don't want to wait!

➤ To leave camp, turn to page 85.

➤ To stay and wait, turn to page 86.

The element of surprise works in your favor at first. Many of the hunters are killed before they can defend themselves. But others manage to grab their guns and hide behind the pile of buffalo skins. As you ride toward them, you feel a bullet rip through your side. You fall from your horse and gasp as you lie dying. Like the buffalo, you will soon be gone from this land.

THE END

To follow another path, turn to page 11.
To read the conclusion, turn to page 101.

You mount your horse and gallop out of camp. You ride for hours through land as familiar to you as your tepee. As you cross a small stream, you notice movement and noise near the bank. White settlers are filling buckets with water. More settlers coming to take whatever they want from your land!

Your hand slowly slides to your gun. But you hesitate. It is not too late to return to camp and wait.

➤ *To put your gun away and return to the camp, turn to page 86.*

➤ *To attack, turn to page 95.*

You must be patient. Waiting is difficult, but it is something you must do.

In spring 1876, Sitting Bull once again calls the band together. "I am leaving for war council," Sitting Bull says. "Stay here and wait for word from me."

For days, you can't eat or sleep. You are too concerned about the coming war. Then people in your camp begin falling sick, one by one.

Early one morning, you are awakened by a shout. A rider gallops to you, breathless.

"Sitting Bull has called you to the large gathering of Lakota and your allies the Cheyenne and Arapaho," the messenger says. "Will you come?"

"There has been sickness in the camp," you reply slowly. "The sick people need strong warriors to guard them."

"I must tell Sitting Bull what you wish to do," the messenger says.

➤ *To stay and guard the camp, turn to page **88**.*

➤ *To go to the gathering, turn to page **89**.*

"Tell the great chief that I must protect the camp," you say. "I will come when the people get well." The messenger jumps back on his horse and rides away.

Turn to page 96.

Religious ceremonies were an important part of American Indian culture.

You leave your band behind and travel to where Sitting Bull is camped near the Little Bighorn River. You are honored that your chief has asked you to join him. There must be thousands of people here.

Sitting Bull leads a ceremony called the Sun Dance. During the ceremony, Sitting Bull cuts his arms 100 times. "It is a sign of his sacrifice to his people," you whisper to yourself.

Turn the page.

After the ceremony, Sitting Bull speaks to the others in the camp. "I had a great vision during the Sun Dance," he says. "I saw bluecoat soldiers falling into our camp like grasshoppers falling from the sky." You and others are inspired by the idea that the white soldiers will be defeated.

The great chief Crazy Horse is in the crowd. He too is inspired by Sitting Bull's vision. Crazy Horse turns to the assembled warriors. "We must attack quickly!" he shouts. "It is time!" Then, he turns to you. "Will you join me, warrior?" he asks.

→ To follow Crazy Horse, go to page **91**.

→ To stay in the camp with Sitting Bull, turn to page **94**.

Crazy Horse fought to keep his land free of white settlers.

You don't have to think about it. "Yes!" you say. A few days later, Crazy Horse leads you and other warriors to Rosebud Creek.

A group of soldiers is camped there. You and the other warriors gallop into their camp, your guns firing.

Turn the page.

The terrified soldiers scurry to grab their weapons. Even though you surprised the soldiers, they fight fiercely. Many warriors fall to the soldiers' bullets.

But the soldiers finally give up. Victory! You let out whoops of joy and fire your gun as the soldiers ride away.

You return to the camp at the Little Bighorn River. That night, you feast and tell stories of the battle.

A few days later, a messenger rides into camp. He tells you that the sickness in your band is getting worse. Someone needs to protect your band from the soldiers. Should you return to your home camp?

→ To go back to your camp, go to page **93**.

→ To stay with Sitting Bull and Crazy Horse, turn to page **94**.

You are worried about your family. "I must go back to my people," you explain to Crazy Horse. "I will return as soon as my people are well again." You ride until you reach your camp. Once you're there, you realize that your people's situation has grown worse.

Turn to page 96.

You stay in Sitting Bull's camp. Word comes to you that the bluecoat soldiers are on the move toward the camp.

The next morning, you are awakened by shouts. You rush from your tepee to see a huge cloud of dust rushing toward camp. The soldiers! You grab your gun and join the other warriors just as an army of soldiers ride into camp.

The air is filled with clouds of dust and the sound of thundering hooves, screams, and rifle fire as you attack. The soldiers are taking the women and children as prisoners. What do you do next?

➻ To try to save the women and children, turn to page **97**.

➻ To keep fighting, turn to page **98**.

Quietly, you pull out your gun and take aim. At that moment, your horse steps on a branch. You quickly fire, but your horse loses his footing. Your shot goes wildly in the air. The man at the creek shouts and fires his gun at you. The bullet hits you in the stomach. You slowly slide off your horse onto the ground. Soon, a crowd of whites gathers around you, shouting and poking you. It is not the kind of death you wanted. But it is death, just the same.

THE END

To follow another path, turn to page 11.
To read the conclusion, turn to page 101.

A feeling of helplessness washes over you. Almost everyone in camp is either sick or dying. But you won't leave them to die alone.

You begin to feel dizzy and confused. Some time later, you hear shouts and the sound of galloping horses. Then you hear gunfire! You stagger out of your tepee, gun in hand, but you are very weak. Blue uniformed soldiers on horseback fill the camp. You sway and then fall to the ground. The sickness kills you before the soldiers get the chance.

THE END

To follow another path, turn to page 11.
To read the conclusion, turn to page 101.

In the Battle of Little Bighorn, about 650 soldiers fought against more than 2,500 American Indian warriors.

You charge up the hill toward the soldiers who have the women and children. You manage to shoot several soldiers.

"Run!" you shout to the women and children. Suddenly your horse stumbles and falls, throwing you to the ground. You feel a sharp pain through your chest. You sink to the ground. At least you saved the children, you think, as your mind goes dark.

THE END

To follow another path, turn to page 11.
To read the conclusion, turn to page 101.

With a shout, you get the attention of several warriors. They see the women and children in danger and rush to help.

Relieved, you turn and join a group of warriors chasing a small group of soldiers. With guns firing and the air buzzing with the sound of arrows, you force the soldiers to the river. Many soldiers drown in the fast-flowing water.

You notice a soldier with long yellow hair. You can tell he is the leader. Many warriors, including you, want the honor of killing him. Finally, someone does. One by one, all of the soldiers are killed.

The battle is over. You are covered with blood, sweat, and dirt. But you are alive.

George Custer was the yellow-haired man who led a group of U.S. soldiers in the Battle of Little Bighorn.

"This is a great victory for the Lakota!" you shout. You are proud of the bravery and courage your people showed. Now, maybe once and for all, the soldiers will leave your people in peace.

THE END

To follow another path, turn to page 11.
To read the conclusion, turn to page 101.

The period of westward expansion saw thousands of pioneers settle in the West.

CHAPTER 5

The End of the Wild West

The great westward expansion lasted only about 40 years. It began in the 1840s, when the first big groups of settlers pushed west. In the years that followed, pioneers flooded the West by the tens of thousands.

In 1845, magazine editor John L. O'Sullivan coined the phrase "Manifest Destiny." The phrase described the feeling that expanding westward was the United States' God-given right.

In 1861, the Civil War put Manifest Destiny out of the minds of many people. This war was fought between northern states, or the Union, and southern states, or the Confederacy. But after the war, thousands of Southerners went west, hoping to find a new life.

The Transcontinental Railroad opened up the West even more. People could travel from east to west in two weeks instead of six months. Small towns soon sprang up along the railroad routes.

Texas ranchers hired cowboys to move herds of cattle north to towns served by the railroad. The Chisholm Trail from southern Texas to Abilene, Kansas, was the main cattle route. From there, trains carried cattle to markets in the East.

Hundreds of small towns were built along the railroad route.

As white settlers moved west, they entered land that belonged to American Indians. The U.S. government made treaties with American Indians to share the land. But one by one, the government broke the treaties.

Some Indians fought to keep control of their land. The conflict worsened when gold was found in the Black Hills. Settlers poured into the area, which had been set aside for the Sioux Indians. To fight back, Sitting Bull and Crazy Horse led their tribes in the Battle of Little Bighorn in 1876. It was the largest military victory for the American Indians. But their triumph was short-lived. By the late 1880s, American Indians were forced onto reservations throughout the West.

Thousands of wagon wheels carved deep ruts into the Oregon Trail that can still be seen today.

By 1890, most people considered the West to be settled. The period of westward expansion came to an end.

In just 20 years, the West's population grew from about 7 million to more than 16 million. Pioneers settled in almost every state, building farms and starting towns.

People who were part of the great westward movement left their mark on America. The pioneer spirit — inventiveness, strength, and a hunger for adventure — is still a part of American culture today.

TIME LINE

1803 — In the Louisiana Purchase, the U.S. government buys 530 million acres of land from France for $15 million.

1841 — The first wagon train of pioneers crosses the Rocky Mountains.

1843 — A group of about 1,000 pioneers leaves Independence, Missouri, on the Oregon Trail.

1845 — Magazine editor John L. O'Sullivan is the first to describe the idea of Manifest Destiny.

1848 — On January 24, James Marshall discovers gold near Sutter's Mill in California.

1849 — More than 80,000 gold miners flood into California's gold fields.

1850 — California becomes a state.

1859 — Oregon becomes a state.

1860 — Abraham Lincoln is elected president.

1861 — The Civil War begins.

1865 — The Civil War ends; construction on the transcontinental railroad begins.

1867 — Cowboys drive cattle from Texas up the Chisholm Trail to Abilene, Kansas, in the first cattle drive.

1868 — The U.S. government creates the Great Sioux Reservation in Dakota Territory.

1869 — The Transcontinental Railroad is completed at Promontory Summit, Utah.

1875 — The U.S. government offers to buy the Black Hills for $6 million. The Lakota refuse the offer.

1876 — On June 17, Crazy Horse and 500 warriors make a surprise attack on U.S. troops on the Rosebud River. On June 25, Lakota defeated George Custer's soldiers at the Battle of Little Bighorn.

1877 — Crazy Horse surrenders to General George Crook at Fort Robinson, Nebraska. Later that year, he is killed by a soldier when he resists being put into jail.

1890 — Sitting Bull is shot and killed by Lakota police sent by the U.S. government to arrest him.

OTHER PATHS TO EXPLORE

In this book, you've seen how the events surrounding westward expansion look different from three points of view.

Perspectives on history are as varied as the people who lived it. You can explore other paths on your own to learn more about what happened. Seeing history from many points of view is an important part of understanding it.

Here are some ideas for other westward expansion points of view to explore:

◆ Farmers in the West had to overcome many hardships to build a successful farm. What was life like on a pioneer farm?

◆ American Indians were forced to move to reservations, sometimes far away from their traditional homelands. What would it have been like to adjust to a new home and a new way of life?

◆ After the Civil War, thousands of former slaves moved west, mostly to Kansas. Did they experience the same treatment in the West as they had received in the South?

READ MORE

Gitlin, Marty. *The Battle of the Little Bighorn.* Edina, Minn.: Abdo, 2008.

Moriarty, J. T. *Manifest Destiny: A Primary Source History of America's Territorial Expansion in the 19th Century.* New York: Rosen, 2005.

Renehan, Edward. *The Transcontinental Railroad: The Gateway to the West.* New York: Chelsea House, 2007.

Schaefer, Ted. *Westward to the Pacific: From the Trail of Tears to the Transcontinental Railroad.* Chicago: Heinemann Library, 2007.

INTERNET SITES

FactHound offers a safe, fun way to find Internet sites related to this book. All of the sites on FactHound have been researched by our staff.

109

Here's how:

1. Visit *www.facthound.com*
2. Choose your grade level.
3. Type in this book ID **1429613599** for age-appropriate sites. You may also browse subjects by clicking on letters, or by clicking on pictures and words.
4. Click on the **Fetch It** button.

FactHound will fetch the best sites for you!

GLOSSARY

baron (BA-ruhn) — a man of great power or influence in some field or activity, such as a business

carcass (KAR-kuhss) — the body of a dead animal

cholera (KOL-ur-uh) — a dangerous disease that causes severe sickness and diarrhea; cholera is caused by contaminated food or water.

Confederate (kuhn-FED-ur-uht) — a person who banded together with others in the South to oppose the North during the Civil War

expansion (ek-SPAN-shuhn) — the process of making a territory larger

Manifest Destiny (MAN-uh-fest DESS-tuh-nee) — the belief that God gave white Americans the right to take over lands that belonged to other people

reservation (rez-ur-VAY-shuhn) — an area of land set aside by the U.S. government for American Indians

stampede (stam-PEED) — to run in panic

transcontinental (transs-kon-tuh-NEN-tuhl) — crossing a continent

BIBLIOGRAPHY

Billington, Ray Allen. *Westward Expansion: A History of the American Frontier.* New York: Macmillan, 1949.

Eaton, Herbert. *The Overland Trail to California in 1852.* New York: Putnam, 1974.

Gard, Wayne. *The Chisholm Trail.* Norman, Okla.: University of Oklahoma Press, 1954.

Gray, Arthur Amos. *Men Who Built the West.* Freeport, N.Y.: Books for Libraries Press, 1972.

Malinowski, Sharon, et al, eds. *Gale Encyclopedia of Native American Tribes.* Detroit: Gale, 1998.

Standing Bear, Luther. *My People, the Sioux.* New York: Houghton Mifflin, 1928.

Sturtevant, William C., ed. *Handbook of North American Indians. Vol. 13: The Plains.* Washington, D.C.: Smithsonian Institution.

Wexler, Sanford, ed. *Westward Expansion: An Eyewitness History.* New York: Facts on File, 1991.

Wheeler, Keith, and the editors of Time-Life Books. *The Railroaders. The Old West.* New York: Time-Life Books, 1973.

INDEX